NINJAS

WARRIORS AROUND THE WORLD

NINJAS

GREG ROZA

Britannica
Educational Publishing

Published in 2017 by Britannica Educational Publishing (a trademark of Encyclopædia Britannica, Inc.) in association with The Rosen Publishing Group, Inc.
29 East 21st Street, New York, NY 10010

Distributed exclusively by Rosen Publishing.
To see additional Britannica Educational Publishing titles, go to rosenpublishing.com.

First Edition

Britannica Educational Publishing
J.E. Luebering: Executive Director, Core Editorial
Anthony L. Green: Editor, Compton's by Britannica

Rosen Publishing
Heather Moore Niver: Editor
Nelson Sá: Creative Director
Matt Cauli: Designer
Cindy Reiman: Photography Manager
Heather Moore Niver: Photo Researcher

Library of Congress Cataloging-in-Publication Data

Names: Roza, Greg, author.
Title: Ninjas / Greg Roza.
Description: New York : Britannica Educational Publishing in association with Rosen Educational Services, [2017] | Series: Warriors around the world | Includes bibliographical references and index. | Audience: Grades 5–8.
Identifiers: LCCN 2016024165| ISBN 9781508103769 (library bound) | ISBN 9781508104360 (pbk.) | ISBN 9781508103028 (6-pack)
Subjects: LCSH: Ninja—Juvenile literature.
Classification: LCC UB271.J3 R69 2017 | DDC 355.5/48—dc23
LC record available at https://lccn.loc.gov/2016024165

Manufactured in China

Photo credits: Cover, p. 3 Fotokvadrat/Shutterstock.com; pp. 7, 22 (inset), 33, 37, 42 Pictures from History/Bridgeman Images; p. 10 © charistoone-images/Alamy Stock Photo; p. 12 © MCLA Collection/Alamy Stock Photo; p. 14 © ZUMA Press, Inc./Alamy Stock Photo; p. 15 (inset) © Jandrie Lombard/Alamy Stock Photo; p. 16 JTB Photo/Universal Images Group/Getty Images; p. 17 Rolls Press/Popperfoto/Getty Images; p. 19 © Chris Willson/Alamy Stock Photo; p. 23 (inset) Print Collector/Hulton Archive/Getty Images; pp. 24-25 © Jeremy Sutton-Hibbert/Alamy Stock Photo; pp. 26-27 Toshifumi Kitamura/AFP/Getty Images; p. 30 Werner Forman/Universal Images Group/Getty Images; p. 32 John S Lander/LightRocket/Getty Images; pp. 34-35 (inset) dotshock/Shutterstock.com; p. 38 redplus2307/iStock/Thinkstock; p. 39 Nattapol Sritongcom/Shutterstock.com; p. 41(inset) ©AAAC/TopFoto/The Image Works; interior pages border images © iStockphoto.com/edfuentesg (ninja), SS1001/Shutterstock.com (sword); pp. 15, 22, 23, 34, 35, 41 (background) © iStockphoto.com/1001nights.

CONTENTS

INTRODUCTION

In a modern world where action films and exciting video games are so popular, it's no wonder that ninjas have established an iconic presence in popular culture. With their traditional black clothes, enigmatic masks, and extraordinary weaponry, ninjas are surrounded by an aura of deadly mystery. This trait stems from their historical presence as figures who conducted missions based on secrecy, spying, and sometimes assassinations. While many facts about ninjas have been clouded by stories and modern entertainment trends, they were real warriors in Japan hundreds of years ago.

The original ninjas were members of secret societies formed in Japan prior to 1500. At that time, warlords and their followers ruled Japan. For security reasons, various clans trained individuals as spies, saboteurs, and fighters to engage in what would be called covert action today. These stealthy soldiers were called many things. We know them as ninjas, although that term did not appear until the twentieth century.

Ninjas were trained in the art of ninjutsu—another newer term. Unlike other martial arts, ninjutsu doesn't focus solely on hand-to-hand combat and the use of weapons. Ninjutsu is a discipline based more on the methods of espionage and treachery. The original term for ninjutsu was *shinobi no jutsu*, which can be translated as "skills of stealth and perseverance." Any man or woman who helped spy on or disrupt the enemy could have been considered a ninja. Professional ninjas studied ninjutsu and mastered its many useful talents, particularly those that aid in spying. Ninjas were

わつくり立の
月上をきくき
平らくてれ信干様

ならほ師

高城ましこの月らつて
不不るもとはてて
すろなろみきの
山らふきことて

This is a page from an eighteenth-century collection of hand-colored illustrations of Japanese trades and customs. The two men in the illustration are shinobi, or ninjas.

also scouts, arsonists, thieves, soldiers, and to a lesser extent assassins. Today, ninja tactics are considered an early form of guerrilla warfare. Modern military tacticians still follow principles found in many ninjutsu manuals.

Modern myths often say that ninjas were outlaw enemies of the samurai, who were military leaders employed by powerful generals.

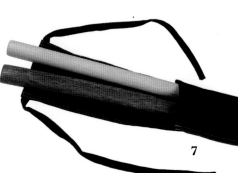

However, records from long ago describe the ninja as a functional part of a warlord's reign, and they often worked side by side for the same generals. In fact, some samurai also acted as ninjas. Together, ninjas and samurai helped defend their clan from enemies. The samurai were military leaders and very visible. The ninjas were often soldiers who worked behind the scenes and in disguise.

Ninja societies were outlawed under the Tokugawa shogunate in the seventeenth century. The art of ninjutsu was all but forgotten over the years. The ninjas' true purpose and methods were clouded by myths and legends. They became shadowy figures in black clothing and masks, flourishing exotic weapons and killing silently. While these stories are rooted in historical facts, they don't give a complete perspective of one of history's more mysterious warriors.

Today, the myths and legends still dominate the public's perception of ninjas. At the movies, viewers love to watch ninjas go to war. They appear in video games, cartoons, and popular literature. Some modern ninjutsu "grand masters" claim to be direct descendants of ninja clans, but this is highly unlikely. Only carefully guarded scrolls, some of which have only just recently been examined and translated by Western scholars, reveal the true nature of the ninjas and how they served their leaders.

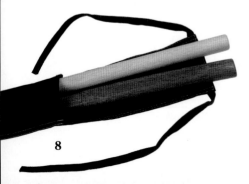

CHAPTER 1
THE HISTORY OF NINJAS

During the fourteenth century, which is considered Japan's medieval period, Japan was not unified under a single government. Many clans were at war with each other. Feudal warlords sent armies led by generals and samurai to defend their clan and crush their enemies. They also hired ninjas trained in the deadly arts of ninjutsu to spy on and, if needed, kill their enemies.

Ninjas were known by many names, depending on the type of ninja as well as the location where they operated. In official records dating from the fourteenth century, ninjas were most commonly known as *shinobi*. Eventually this changed to *shinobi no mono*, which translates to "a man of perseverance and stealth."

CHINESE ORIGINS

So far, the earliest reference to ninjas in historical Japanese documents occurred in the late fourteenth century. However, many ninja resources contain origin stories that predate this time by hundreds of years. Sources often disagree, so it's difficult to say for sure how or where ninjutsu originated. However, there's good evidence that ninjutsu was born in China.

Espionage and spying had been used as warfare tactics for hundreds of years before the shinobi appeared in Japan. Several ninja

Sun Tzu was a military specialist who lived during the sixth century BCE. His work The Art of War *is widely considered a masterpiece on the topic of warfare.*

manuals address the Chinese origins of their methods and beliefs. Ninjutsu manuals often mention tactics first recorded by Chinese general Sun Tzu's classic essay on warfare, *The Art of War*. Sun Tzu's five types of spies are often mirrored in ninja manuals. There's more proof that many ninja strategies were first used in ancient China. These range from espionage and warfare tactics to specialized weaponry and incendiary devices.

IGA AND KOKA

Before the era dominated by warring clans and power-hungry warlords, the ninjas were established in a wild, rocky area near Kyoto. This area was made up of the provinces of Iga (now part of Mie Prefecture) and Koka (now part of Shiga Prefecture). This rugged country became a hiding place for criminals and soldiers who had lost in battle. It was here that ninjutsu has its beginning.

Some stories and records say that Chinese soldiers fled to Iga and Koka long ago, bringing ancient knowledge with them. Over the years, the ninjas of Iga and Koka trained in secret, perfecting their many techniques and methods. In time they developed the art of ninjutsu, fostering the skills and passing them on to new generations.

References to ninjas became more common in records from the fifteenth and sixteenth centuries. This era is known as the Sengoku period, or the Warring States period. At this time, many clans fought for power and territory. Warlords known as daimyo waged constant

This painting depicts the beautiful yet rugged Iga province where the Hanzo clan originated.

war on neighboring clans, hoping to conquer them all. This era was also dominated by internal conflicts, and a daimyo had to watch out for enemies in their own ranks. Warriors from Iga and Koka continually impressed daimyo with their ferocity in battle, and also with their creativity and stealth. Daimyos began employing ninjas as spies and saboteurs. Eventually, shinobi became an official, although secretive, position in many Japanese armies.

THE HANZO CLAN

Much of what we know about ninjas come from family records, often in the form of scrolls. Recorded by famous warriors, samurai, and shinobi, they often describe the family history, as well as essential tactics in war and espionage. Military and government records mention many of the same ninjas mentioned in the scrolls.

Perhaps the most commonly known ninja from history is Hattori Hanzo. Hanzo was a well-known samurai and shinobi, and possibly the main author of the *Shinobi Hiden*, although it may also have been his father. Hanzo was just one individual in a long line of famous shinobi. The Hanzo clan in the Iga province had long been known as fierce warriors and dedicated ninjas.

Of all the historical ninjas, Hattori Hanzo's name may be most recognizable for Westerners due to its use in popular media. Characters with the name Hattori Hanzo have appeared in numerous movies. In 2003, a character with that name appeared in *Kill Bill*, a film by director and kung fu movie fan Quentin Tarantino. In this case, Hattori

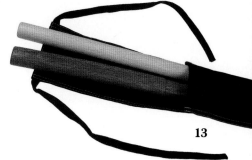

Modern depictions of ninjas are usually silent killers in black clothing. In Kill Bill, *Hanzo's character is friendly and likeable.*

owns a sushi bar in Okinawa, but he is also a legendary sword maker. This is just one more case of modern movies changing the facts of history when it comes to the ninjas.

THE FALL OF THE SHINOBI

In 1551, a daimyo named Oda Nobunaga succeeded where all other daimyo had failed. He claimed control of the Oda clan when his father died that year. By 1560, Nobunaga had unified the Owari Province, which was in close proximity to Iga and Koka. Nobunaga was the fiercest of the daimyos at the time, and his military power initiated the move toward unification of Japan under a single government.

FEMALE NINJAS

The idea of a female counterpart to the ninja is a modern conception. It's safe to say that ninjutsu was practiced mainly by men, but were there female ninjas?

Much like the common men of the period, women spies could be used to gain information on an enemy warlord, either by finding work in his headquarters or by befriending those close to him. One record explains how to use women and children to create fake families, perhaps for use in hostage situations. This often turned out badly for the fake family.

So far, just one description of a specific female shinobi has been discovered. It appears in the *Bansenshukai*. The text describes a woman of the Edo period (1603–1863) whose abilities were so strong that no other male ninja could rival her. Following ninja traditions, she passed her knowledge on to a male ninja.

Today, female ninjas are just as popular as male ninjas. They appear in movies, television shows, comic books, and video games.

As wars and distrust between clans diminished, so too did the importance of ninjas. Rulers no longer needed spies to find out what their enemies were doing and planning. In time, references to shinobi and ninjutsu disappeared from military records. The era of the shinobi had ended.

This statue of Oda Nobunaga stands at Kiyosu Castle in Kiyosu, Japan. He took control of the Oda clan in 1551.

THE RISE OF THE NINJA

For many years, nothing more was recorded about the shinobi. That doesn't mean they were forgotten. They remained alive in oral traditions and in safely guarded scrolls. By the nineteenth century in Japan, public perception of the shinobi had transformed the historical figure to legendary status. It's interesting to note that the term "ninja" was likely never even used during medieval Japan. That term arose later, and with it rose the mythical figure of the deadly and mysterious ninja assassin.

The 1964 Olympics were held in Tokyo, Japan. In this photograph, the Japanese athletes wave to fans during the closing ceremony.

Some stories say Japanese soldiers used ninja tactics during World War II. Another story says the 1964 Japanese Olympic team trained in ninjutsu in order to win. Today, ninjas have become mythical, entertaining characters based on historic figures, much like pirates and Vikings. Writers and moviemakers have instilled superhuman qualities in the ninjas, transforming them into larger-than-life figures.

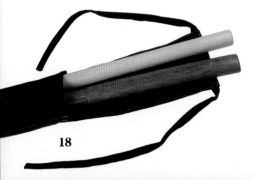

CHAPTER 2
NINJUTSU

When you hear the word "ninjutsu," do you picture ninjas wearing black, sneaking through the shadows, throwing shuriken (throwing stars) and bearing deadly swords? If so, you might be surprised to hear that there are few references to black clothing in ninja manuals, and more surprised to hear that shuriken have yet to be connected to the ninja. This demonstrates the basic problem with our understanding of the ninja today. Much of what we know is clouded by myths, stories, and half-truths.

The town of Iga Ueno, shown here, was well known as a training ground for ninjas, some of whom served in the military.

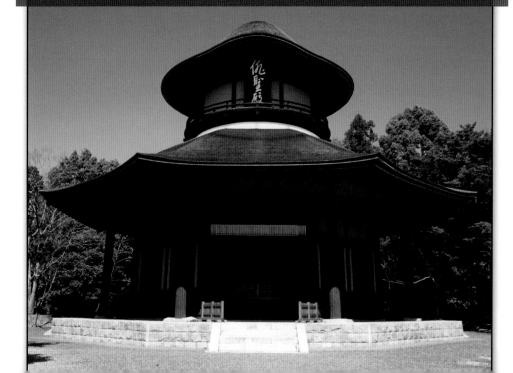

Ninjutsu is different from the martial arts, which focus on hand-to-hand combat and weaponry. Ninjutsu certainly encompasses martial arts skills, but it involves much more. At its core, ninjutsu was the art of espionage. In fact, many ninja manuals taught that ninjas should flee from fights. It was often more important for them to return to their leaders with information rather than engage an enemy in battle.

Ninjutsu developed in an era of warfare, and it served an important military role. Once the skills of Iga and Koka warriors became common knowledge, many warlords hired ninjas to serve in their militaries. Some ninjas were regular soldiers. Others were samurai, criminals, or failed generals. Regardless of their rank in society, those who practiced ninjutsu were valued as masters of espionage.

HISTORIC TEXTS

Much of what we know about ninjas and ninjutsu comes from military records and ninja manuals. Most are copies of originals that no longer exist. Some of these documents have only recently been translated into English. Documents, some in the form of scrolls, have been handed down over the generations, and not all families are willing to share them. This has helped the true facts surrounding the ninja to remain hidden for many years.

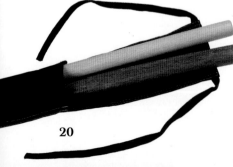

In recent years, English historian Antony Cummins has become the leading Western scholar of ninjas and samurai. Thanks to Cummins and

and the Historical Ninjutsu Research Team, the Western world is now gaining a better understanding of who the ninjas really were. Cummins has examined numerous documents, but four stand out from the rest.

One of the oldest of the sources Cummins has examined is the *Shinobi Hiden* (The Secret Traditions of the Shinobi). This is a training manual written in the 1560s, possibly by the samurai and ninja Hattori Hanzo. The *Bansenshukai* (The Book of the Ninja) is a well-known ninja manual, written in 1676. It contains eleven books on ninjutsu and military strategy. Other important sources include the *Shoninki* (1681) and the *Gunpo Jiyoshun* (1612), both of which contain ninja tactics and directions.

THE ART OF ESPIONAGE

At its heart, ninjutsu is the art of espionage. Ninja manuals offer specific circumstances and the proper methods for gaining an advantage over enemies. This could include the best way to eavesdrop on a conversation, how to gain the confidence of enemy servants, how to sneak into a heavily guarded location, and much more.

Sun Tzu listed the five types of spies in *The Art of War*. These include local spies, internal spies, turned spies (former enemies), doomed spies (those intended to die during a mission), and living spies (those who gain knowledge and return). This list had a great influence on other military leaders in Asia, and it helps shed light on ninjutsu. There wasn't just one kind of ninja. Rather, they were trained to fulfill

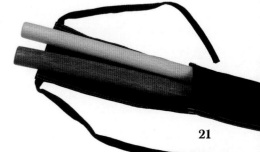

SAMURAI VERSUS NINJA?

Legends often say that samurai and ninjas were sworn enemies, but that's far from the truth. Samurai and ninjas formed two separate branches in the military, and they often worked closely together.

Warlords set up networks that included ninjas in key places for a large number of reasons. These networks included a hierarchy of shinobi ranks under the warlord's

This painting from sometime in the 1850s by artist Utagawa Kunikazu depicts a conflict between two samurai and a ninja.

control. Although some shinobi played a role in the public eye, most were hiding in plain sight. Some worked in secret hundreds of miles away as a soldier in the ranks of an enemy. Others worked close to the warlord.

Samurai, however, were much like the knights of medieval England. They were professional soldiers who owned

Samurai warriors, one of which is depicted here, were highly respected members of medieval Japanese society. Ninjas often preferred to remain hidden from the public eye.

land and lived by a strict code. Yet, it's important to note that the term "samurai" indicated a high rank in society, while "shinobi" was merely a job title. A shinobi was an employee who had a specific set of skills, and it had nothing to do with social class. Many samurai, including Hattori Hanzo, were also talented ninjas. Some records show that shinobi were often placed in charge of samurai.

many needs under many circumstances. Ninjutsu tactics encompassed all forms of espionage.

A single ninja might specialize as one type of spy, or a ninja may have many skills. Ninjas might have been adept at starting fires, infiltrating an enemy's castle, or swordsmanship—or all of these and more. The best ninjas trained in as many arts as they could, thus mastering the art of ninjutsu.

IT'S A FAMILY THING

There's little mention of ninja schools in the historical records of Japan. It's most likely that individual families developed their own ninjutsu styles and passed them down to their descendants. In this way, the ninjutsu "schools" were more like family traditions. These families taught many battle skills, including horsemanship, weaponry, and hand-to-hand combat. Ninjutsu, however, offered a much larger array of talents, all designed for one main purpose: espionage.

Professional ninjas went through tough training from an early age. Their fathers and perhaps other family

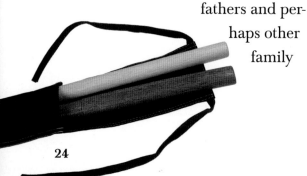

members often taught them the secrets of ninjutsu and other arts. After mastering ninjutsu, a master would teach his craft to another student. Ancient arts were passed down by word of mouth, and few records were kept at first. Later, as the shinobi came to importance, some famous ninjas finally recorded the histories of their clans.

MODERN NINJUTSU

Despite the records we do have, we still don't know all there is to know about ninjutsu. We know ninjutsu was practiced during the Warring States period of Japan's history, and we know it was

Most modern ninjutsu schools teach self-defense, martial arts, and weaponry, rather than the ancient arts of espionage.

nearly abandoned in the years that followed. Today, several ninja schools claim to have a direct link to the ninja families of the past. Are their claims legitimate?

Modern ninjutsu schools began opening in the 1970s and 1980s. They are rising in popularity today. Many ninjutsu schools offer a well-rounded martial arts program including karate, jujutsu, judo, and other modern martial arts. Some also teach martial arts that were in use before modern systems replaced them. Ninjutsu schools also offer a taste of the authentic ninja curriculum, including training in stealth and spying. The resurgence of interest in ninjutsu has spread around the globe.

In 1978, Japanese martial artist Masaaki Hatsumi founded the Bunjikan ninjutsu school, which is still open today. Over the years, many others have followed in Hatsumi's footsteps by starting their own schools and forms of ninjutsu.

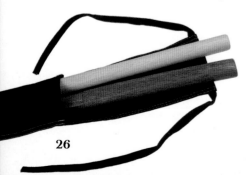

Masaaki Hatsumi, the grandmaster of the Bunjikan ninjutsu school, sits top center in this photograph. Some grandmasters believe they are descendants of the fourteenth- and fifteenth-century shinobi families.

Some ninja "grandmasters" claim to be descendants of the shinobi families of the fourteenth and fifteenth centuries. Others are skeptical of these claims. More ninja scrolls are sure to be discovered and translated in the years to come. Perhaps they will offer us more information to connect modern ninjutsu schools to ancient clans. At the moment, however, there's no evidence to support lineage claims to ninjutsu families of the past.

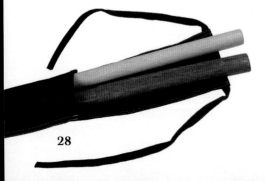

CHAPTER 3
TACTICS AND STRATEGIES

As we've learned, historical records show that the ninjas were prepared for just about every situation. Their tools and weaponry were both clever and devious, and this is one facet that modern interpretations of ninjas often focus on. However, not all ninjas were deadly fighters or masters of explosives. Some were regular people who were able to infiltrate enemy locations to gather information.

Military manuals listed the qualities a ninja should have. Some of the more important qualities may surprise you. Ninjas who were witty and good at befriending people were valuable, but being "stupid looking" may have been even more important!

There were two kinds of ninja: the type of skilled ninjas we often picture now, and unskilled ninja who were used for various jobs. Espionage and secrecy—not martial arts and weaponry—are really what the ninjas were all about.

SPYING AND SCOUTING

If there's one thing ninjas were known for, it was spying. The average citizen could serve as shinobi to his or her warlord in many ways. Simply blending in with a warlord's enemies was enough to earn the respect of leaders, as well as the name "ninja."

This print shows a ninja giving a secret hand gesture. Ninjas used codes and secret gestures to prove who they were to fellow ninjas.

Unlike their highly visible samurai counterparts, the shinobi most often hid in plain sight. Costumes and disguises could be employed, but many ninjas wore the clothes typical of the day. Unskilled ninjas were effective in everyday situations.

Ninja documents are filled with spying scenarios. Skilled ninjas were trained to handle any situation, no matter how odd it may sound. How did ninjas sneak into a dark room on a moonlit night? What was the best way to overhear a conversation in a crowded room? Which type of person is most likely to give up information? Ninja manuals had all the answers.

A ninja's skills were also perfect for secretive scouting. Many ninja manuals discuss effective scouting practices and how to benefit from them. Scouts identified gaps and weaknesses in an enemy's defenses. They used a complex system of signals to spread information quickly. Adept ninja scouts could save a warlord from an embarrassing defeat. They could also provide information needed to destroy an enemy.

SABOTAGE

Besides spying on enemies, ninjas were also instructed to disrupt the enemy's plans whenever possible. As in the movies, sabotage could entail plots of murder and property destruction. It wasn't always dramatic. Sometimes all it took was to spread a little misinformation. Other times it had more violent conclusions.

Not only were ninjas clever at mixing and handling explosive chemicals, they were equally skilled at using them to disrupt an enemy. Ninjas

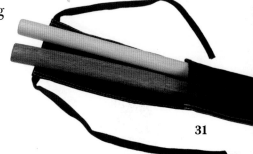

were often called upon to start fires for various reasons, whether it was for a diversion, to destroy property, or to kill enemies. Other forms of sabotage included spreading lies, distributing propaganda, damaging food supplies, and poisoning water supplies.

WARFARE AND ASSASSINATION

Ninjas were often recruited as mercenaries by armies all over Japan. They were well-known as fierce warriors who refused to give up. When ninjas were called on to go into battle with enemies, they often employed guerrilla tactics. These are unconventional methods of warfare that include small armies that commit surprise attacks.

Many ninjas were also used as assassins when the need arose. Contrary to our modern vision of ninjas as merciless killers, assassinations were less common than we might think. The ninja's primary objective was espionage, but at times he was called on to murder key enemy leaders.

This print is by artist Tomioka Eisen (1864–1905). The ninja's special set of skills allowed him to fulfill many roles, including assassin.

THIEVERY

Thievery was another art the ninjas practiced. They were known to steal money and other valuables from enemies. This helped disable the enemy and also added to the warlord's wealth. Some shinobi, samurai, and military leaders stole for their own profit. The ninjas were also sometimes confused with or compared to another figure known as *nusubito*, or thief.

A section of the *Bansenshukai* devoted to burglary mentions ninjas named "dogs," who were talented thieves.

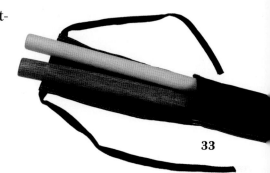

DID NINJAS REALLY WEAR BLACK?

One of the biggest misunderstandings people have about ninjas is that they wore black outfits and hid their faces with black masks. The ninja outfits we think of were a

common style in the time of the ninjas (minus the mask, of course). Ninja manuals address types of clothing and disguise. They mention that black clothing should be worn during a night when there was no moonlight. Some sources say dark blue was a better choice. Although ninjas dressed in black with black masks is a historical fact, thieves used this type of attire more often.

Most ninjas wore typical clothes of the era to avoid drawing attention to themselves. Wearing all black would surely have drawn attention to a ninja, whether it was day or night. Some ninjas were also samurai, and they dressed as samurai would. One report talks of a smaller army wearing white when staging a sneak attack on a much larger force. The ninja army stealthily killed anyone not wearing white.

The real ninjas were not the flashy dressers that appear in ninja movies today. It's safe to say that the ninja in black clothing is a modern interpretation of the historical figure.

Ninjas chose clothing to match their mission. In some circumstances, however, they would have been more noticeable in all black.

CHAPTER 4

EQUIPMENT AND WEAPONS

The greatest ninjas excelled at crafting and using tools and weapons. Every action movie fan knows this. These items were specialized to their needs. Surviving documents from the era—including government records and military manuals—list a wide variety of weapons and devices, including how to make and use them. Some are as simple as fire-making tools. Others, such as explosives and poisons, are far more complex. The greatest ninjas were experts in all of them.

NINJA WEAPONRY

Studying ninjutsu weaponry demonstrates how resourceful the shinobi needed to be. As ninja movies and video games display, ninjas are known for their use of cunning and sometimes unexpected weaponry. Ninjas trained in the use of common weapons, such as katanas, knives, bows and arrows, and bo staffs. Surviving ninjutsu documents describe the mastering of these weapons and more. The best ninjas mastered the typical weaponry skills; some were skilled samurai swordsmen.

In this painting from the 1850s by Utagawa Kuniyoshi (1797–1861), a ninja army attacks a samurai with specialized weapons.

One weapon often associated with ninjas is the shuriken, or throwing star. No movie ninja would be caught without them! So far, however, no historical source has been found to link throwing stars to the ninja. This could change, as the shuriken was used during this medieval era in Japan.

Aside from the typical weaponry of the era, ninjas developed and used some extremely clever and deadly weapons. Each weapon or tool was designed for specific purposes. One of the weapons often associated with ninjas is the shuko, or hand claw. This weapon consisted of a metal plate with four sharp spikes on it, and a strap to secure it to the hand. The shuko was easy to conceal. Ninjas

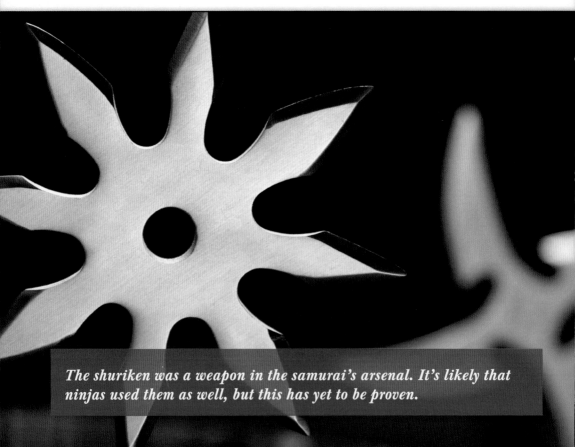

The shuriken was a weapon in the samurai's arsenal. It's likely that ninjas used them as well, but this has yet to be proven.

The kunai was an essential ninja weapon. Originally designed as a masonry trowel, a kunai was easy to conceal. It could be used as a projectile, for hand-to-hand combat, and for scaling walls.

could use it to slash an enemy's face. Similar footwear could be used to scale trees and walls.

The kyoketsu-shoge is a weapon made with a metal ring, a rope, and a barbed knife. A ninja would hold the metal ring and throw the knife. The weapon was deigned to wrap around a victim's neck and cut his or her throat. Other crafty and deadly ninja weapons include blowguns, landmines, and caltrops.

CHEMICALS, POTIONS, AND EXPLOSIVES

The greatest ninjas were also trained how to handle, mix, and use chemicals. They could be considered similar to modern-day pharmacists. They were able to identify and administer drugs to produce desired effects, such as sleepiness, sickness, and death. Ninja manuals contain various recipes, including instructions on how to make energy pills, medicines, poisons, and other helpful potions.

Being able to mix chemicals for potions and poisons, some ninjas could also mix the chemicals needed to create explosives. This was an essential weapon in the ninja arsenal. One particularly sneaky ninja tool was called pocket fire. It consisted of all the materials needed to start a fire or explosion, and it fit inside a pocket. Some contained a flint to make sparks, but some included a chamber containing a burning ember. This ember could be used to keep warm, light torches, and ignite explosives.

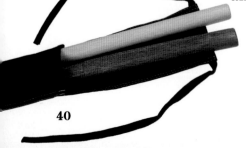

CALTROPS

One of the ninjas' favorite weapons was also their sneakiest. The caltrop is a small spiky device designed to incapacitate invaders and pursuers. It has four sharp points about an inch long each. No matter how you throw a caltrop, it lands with three points forming a tripod and one spike pointing straight up.

Caltrops could be thrown around an area—for example, surrounding a warlord's home—to protect it from intruders (including other ninjas). Invisible at night, caltrops could stop a sneak attack before it even started by sending invaders away with seriously injured feet. They even served as an alarm system. Once someone stepped on it, he or she was sure to yell out in pain and surprise. Caltrops were also used to stop enemies from following ninjas after an attack. They were used to injure and slow down people and horses alike. Some ninjas dragged caltrops on strings to stop anyone from following them.

The earliest recorded use of caltrops appeared in an account written in 331 BCE, which described a battle between Alexander the Great and Persian king Darius III.

CROSSING WALLS AND MOATS

Ninjutsu documents list various ways to get around, over, or under walls. The most common method was by using a ladder. Some ladders were made of rope and could easily be concealed. Others relied on tools in a ninja's possession, such as swords or knives. Large "cloud" ladders were constructed for use in scouting. Ninjas also commonly carried grappling hooks.

Some of the most interesting equipment ninjas were trained in were tools designed to cross moats. At the height of ninja popularity, moats were a

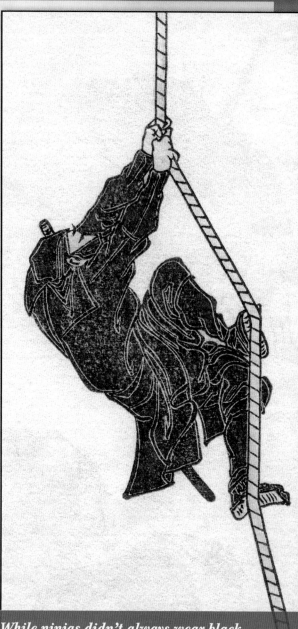

While ninjas didn't always wear black, they did have an extensive skill set and an extensive array of tools and weapons.

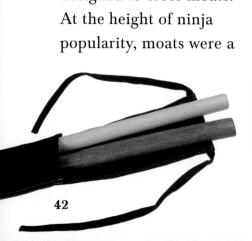

common method of protecting a castle or fortress. It was often vital to cross a moat quickly and silently. A common method was to use a water spider. Sealed leather containers were use to create a ring much like a life preserver, and the user would sit on a leather seat attached to it. Ninjas could also use wooden fins to help push them forward. The water spider was just one example of ninja ingenuity. Snorkels allowed ninjas to travel silently underwater. Other times they constructed light, floating bridges.

CUNNING AND CREATIVE

A ninja's arsenal of weapons and tools is truly impressive. It's this type of creativity and resourcefulness that allowed ninjas to experience such great success during the Sengoku period. It's also what makes them such an interesting topic today. There were few obstacles ninjas could not overcome.

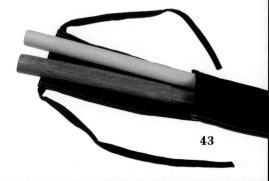

GLOSSARY

arsenal A collection of weapons and military equipment.

assassination The act of killing someone, often someone in power.

cunning Crafty and resourceful.

enigmatic Mysterious or difficult to understand.

espionage Activities done to find out enemy secrets; spying.

feudal Relating to a political system with a lord who allowed people to live on his land if they fought for the lord and protected him.

flint A tool that creates a spark when struck with metal.

guerrilla warfare Unusual military actions, including sabotage and ambushes, carried out by small groups of soldiers.

incapacitate To make someone unable to function in their normal way, usually by injury.

incendiary A substance or weapon used to start a fire.

ingenuity Skill or cleverness in discovering, inventing, or planning.

katana A long, single-edged sword used by samurai.

lineage The people who were in a person's family in the past.

mercenary A professional soldier.

moat A deep, wide trench around the walls of a castle or fortress that is usually filled with water.

perseverance Being able to continue doing something even though it is difficult.

pharmacist A professional trained to mix, prepare, and distribute medications.

prefecture Area that some countries are divided into for local government.

propaganda Ideas that are often exaggerated or false, used to promote a cause or political movement.

saboteur Someone who destroys or damages things on purpose.

shogunate A military ruler of Japan.

tactic Method of arranging and moving forces in combat.

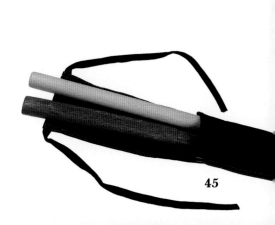

FOR FURTHER READING

Cummins, Antony. *The Book of Ninja: The Bansenshukai*. London, UK: Watkins Publishing, 2013.

Cummins, Antony. *In Search of the Ninja: The Historical Truth of Ninjutsu*. Gloucestershire, UK: The History Press, 2012.

Cummins, Antony. *Samurai and Ninja*. North Clarendon, VT: Tuttle Publishing, 2015.

Gunderson, Jessica. *Ninja: A Guide to the Ancient Assassins*. North Mankato, MN: Capstone, 2011.

Matthews, Rupert. *Ninjas*. New York, NY: Gareth Stevens, 2015.

Matthews, Rupert. *Samurai*. New York, NY: Gareth Stevens, 2015.

Mooney, Carla. *Ninjas*. Edina, MN: ABDO, 2013.

Niz, Xavier W. *Samurai: A Guide to the Feudal Knights*. North Mankato, MN: Capstone, 2011.

WEBSITES

Because of the changing nature of internet links, Rosen Publishing has developed an online list of websites related to the subject of this book. This site is updated regularly. Please use this link to access the list:

http://www.rosenlinks.com/WAW/ninja

INDEX